ALL MANNER OF THINGS

ALL MANNER OF THINGS

LECTIO DIVINA WITH JULIAN OF NORWICH

WILLIAM MENINGER, OCSO

DOVE PUBLISHING

OUR LADY OF GUADALUPE ABBEY

PECOS, NM

2012

Dove Publications

Our Lady of Guadalupe Abbey

PO Box 1080

Pecos, NM 87552

www.dovepublications.org

Cover and text design: Ezra Hubbard

All Manner of Things
William Meninger, OCSO
Dove Publications
Our Lady of Guadalupe Abbey
P.O. Box 1080
Pecos, NM 87552
www.dovepublications.org
ISBN-978-1-931598-19-4

Contents

Introduction

On May 13, 1373 Dame Julian had a series of 16 visions. She spent 20 years meditating on them, that is, using them for her lectio divina. During that interval, Julian the visionary, became Julian the theologian. In a previous book (<u>Julian of Norwich, a Mystic for the 21st Century</u>), I tried to rewrite, chapter by chapter, Julian's book, <u>The Revelations</u> (Shewings) <u>of Divine Love</u>, in an attempt to make its expression more in sync with today's readers. This book has a different purpose. It is intended to provide a source of lectio divina and to be an expression of my own lectio divina on Julian's theology.

I have not covered Julian's book chapter by chapter but have freely taken her ideas, expanding or limiting them, adding scripture texts where helpful and my own reflections. I have also dipped into Julian's contemporaries, the anonymous <u>Cloud of Unknowing</u>, and Richard Hilton's <u>Ladder of Perfection</u>, wherever it was useful. It would seem that Julian also used these sources. There is a sequence of thoughts in her chapters and I have indicated the sources by referring to her work at the beginning of each of my chapters. Any direct quotes from Julian's work is taken from a 17th century translation which is common domain, and may or may not be in quotation marks. Likewise, my quotations from Scripture are not necessarily marked and, in general, are made from memory as was common in the 14th century. The style, some of the vocabulary, and much of the sentence structure may seem a bit awkward. This is because I wished to retain, even in my reflections, the Middle English flavor of Julian's writings.

Much research is being done today in the light of Julian's new and much deserved popularity. Certain Franciscan scholars and even some Jewish influence may come to light through further research, Julian, however, by way of her own personal "lectio divina," makes it all her own even as she does with the Scriptures.

It should never be forgotten that "lectio divina", whether Julian's or our own is the first step on the ladder to contemplation. This book should not be read straight through as something that must be finished. The goal of "lectio" is not to finish a book but to savor it, to allow it to sink from the mind to the heart. Then allow the heart to be touched and raised by a gentle stirring of love for God. We should rest in this love whenever and for as long as we feel inclined. The mind and the heart are companions on the journey to union with God. The heart is roused through love and the mind through wisdom both of which are manifest in the writings by and reflections from Dame Julian.

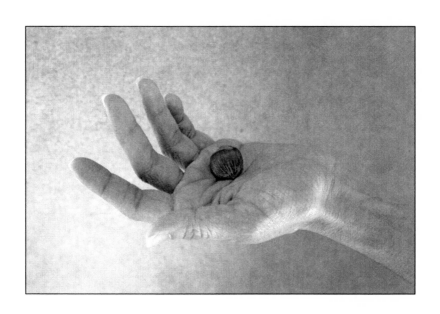

Chapter 1
The Hazelnut

From Shewings- Chapter 5

God is everything that is good and comfortable to us. His love wraps, embraces and envelops us like our clothing. Never will he leave us.

Being is of two kinds: uncreated or created. Uncreated being is God himself. Everything else is created being made by God. Julian was given a vision in her understanding in which she saw all of created being as if it were a small, round ball, the size of a hazelnut in the palm of her hand. She marveled at how it might continue to exist since it was so tiny and fragile. She realized, however, that it would continue to exist because God loved it. All created being, everything that exists from the smallest speck of dust to the vast reaches of the heavens has its being from God and continues in being because of the Blessed Trinity. God the Father made it, God the Son sustains it, and God the Holy Spirit loves it.

By the hazelnut, we are given to realize the insignificance of all created being. Everything was made to love and rest in God, but of itself it is nothing. We are restless and insecure because we seek our rest and security in a hazelnut! God who is almighty, the Father, all wise, the Son, and all loving, the Holy Spirit, is our true rest and the foundation of our being. We were made for God and we cannot rest until we rest in God. We must realize the nothingness of all created being, the hazelnut, especially including ourselves. This is humility, knowing the truth about ourselves, and without it we cannot know the truth about God. And unless we know the truth about God, we can never be secure or find rest.

It is God's joy that we find our rest in him. We cannot rest in anything beneath him. It is only when we lovingly accept our nothingness for God who is everything that our souls can find rest. By the touching of the Holy Spirit, our soul naturally yearns for God and God takes great pleasure in this. It is only in God that we can have everything and we must never ask for less. God's goodness and love embraces all of his creatures and all of his works. The Father created us only for himself, the Son restored us by his blessed passion and death and the Holy Spirit keeps us in his blessed love.

It is the very nature of love or goodness to

be diffusive. Love must share itself. This can be seen as the purpose of creation. God created in order to love. As a part of this hazelnut, we were created to be loved and everything else was created to make love possible. We were not created to be judged, to be punished or even to be held accountable. That love of God which must share itself is infinite, without limits or conditions. When we share in that love, we must also love ourselves and each other so that no one is excluded, overlooked or taken for granted. We can do this because the love of God compels us.

Chapter 2
The Goodness of God

From Shewings- Chapter 5

The goodness of God is our highest prayer. It satisfies our most basic needs. We pray to God in many ways but ultimately these prayers are based on his goodness. His goodness is identical with his love. We pray through our incarnate Lord in his blessed passion and death. All that comes to us from him, God's blessed kindness and eternal life, comes from the goodness of God. We pray through his blessed mother's love and all the help we receive from her. This too, comes from the goodness of God. We pray through the holy cross on which Jesus died and all the strength and help we receive from the cross. And this comes from the goodness of God. Likewise, all the help that we have from our favorite saints, the friendship of all the company of heaven, comes from God's goodness. It pleases God that we seek him and pay him tribute through all these means as long as we understand that he is the goodness behind them all.

The goodness of God is, indeed, our highest

prayer and satisfies our every need. It brings life to the soul and makes it grow strong in grace and virtue. It is for us the most natural thing in the world and, at the same time, is the most available grace. Because of his love for our soul, made in his own image, God does not hesitate to serve our simplest physical needs.

As the body is clad in clothing and the flesh in skin, and the bones in the flesh, and the heart in the whole of it, so are we, body and soul, clad and enclosed in the goodness, the love, of God. Our physical being may waste and wear away but God's goodness is ever near to us. Of all the things that our heart may cling to, God is most pleased when our soul clings to his goodness. This is what brings the soul most swiftly to its fullest completion in God.

We are so totally beloved by God, that it surpasses all our understanding. This is why we, by God's grace and with our spiritual eye, marvel in the contemplation of his unspeakable love and goodness. Because of this we may reverently ask of God whatever we will, knowing that our natural will is to love God as his will is to love us. We will never cease from this willing until we have him in fullness of joy.

The two principal faculties of our soul, our intellect and will, are directed toward knowing and loving God. This knowing and loving God humbles the soul, fills us with reverential fear and with charity for all men and women on earth.

In the spiritual journey and in our life of prayer, there is a standard pattern that we follow over and over again but on different levels. It begins with the virtue of humility which is the foundation of all the virtues. Humility is simply knowing the truth about ourselves. This truth sets us free. It concerns not only our wretchedness, sinfulness and failures but touches on our very nature as created being, our essential nothingness, and our inability of ourselves to come into existence or to sustain ourselves in existence without the help of God. This help from God is also a part of our truth and hence is also a part of our humility. The more profound our awareness of our feebleness, the more profoundly are we led to realize our dependence on God. The finger of God touches our soul, our spiritual eye is opened, and we are given to see God's love and care. This deepens our humility and deepens our love for God. We struggle and pray and strive for the virtue of humility, aided, of course, by God's grace. This step in the journey, going from humility to charity, is given to us without any effort. It is pure grace, a free gift from God. We receive it passively. It does not come from our efforts; we do not merit or deserve it. It is simply given.

The proof of the pudding is in the eating. There is no way to prove this step from humility to charity except by experiencing it or by receiving testimony from those who have experienced it. Certainly the most noble, the highest, the most beautiful human being to follow this pattern from humility to love is our Lady St. Mary. Because of her sinlessness, there is a difference in her approach. She does not begin with her sins. She has none. She begins with her soul magnifying the Lord and rejoicing in him. Our Lady was able to behold the greatness of the Lord. Thus was she filled with a reverential fear by which she saw herself so little and so low, so simple and so poor. This filled her with humility and, grounded in this humility, she was endowed with grace and all manner of virtues, surpassing all of God's creatures. The Lord sees her as she images himself. He regards her lowliness, her humility and rewards her by doing great things for her. He exalts her lowliness by making her the mother of his son, Jesus Christ. Thus it was that the divinity of the Godhead entered into union with the human race. Thus it is that we too are called, when God regards our humility, to be bearers of Christ and one with the Father in the graciousness of the Holy Spirit.

Chapter 3
The Ability to Love God

From Shewings- Chapter 9

The ability to love God is given to every Christian and is the greatest gift we could ever have. Some people do have lesser gifts for the service of the Church but these have value only to the extent that they are coupled with charity. This is why St. Paul tells us that we could have all manner of gifts, including speaking the tongues of angels, the power of prophecy, or enough faith to move mountains but have not love; we are just noisy gongs or clanging cymbals. We are nothing. If we have charity, however, something that is available to all Christians, we have God who is all in all.

Love is given to us, not independently as an individual, but in harmony of our union with each other in the body of Christ. The life of mankind is found in its unity with each other and with God. God is in each of us as when we love one another for his sake. Thus it is not the ability to perform miracles or have visions that makes one special. Rather it is the love of God and charity toward one another. To love one another is to love God, for God is in us whom he has made. This should bring us great comfort.

God is love and where love is, there is God. God does not have to be sought; he simply has to be practiced. As love, God is always reaching out, seeking, bonding or, as Julian says, oneing. This love which is God, permeates the universe, supporting it, holding it in existence. It is pleased and pleasing. God takes joy in himself and in all that he does. Even if all created being is nothing more than a hazelnut, as Julian saw it, it is beloved of God and of infinite worth. This applies not only to the whole of created existence but to every smallest part of it. Jesus assures us that his Father is aware of the movements of the tiniest sparrow.

That very love which the Father has for the Son, he has for all of creation made through the Son, imaged by him and the reflection of his infinite wisdom. The Holy Spirit who is God, is the love which by the diffusion of his goodness sustains the world. This love is the power of the Father, the wisdom of the Son and the goodness of the Holy Spirit. And it is ours!

Chapter 4
The Ground of Our Beseeching

From Shewings- Chapter 10

We are so blind and ignorant that we do not seek God until he has actually found us and shows himself to us. Once we do see him, by his grace, we are stirred by that very grace with the desire to see him even more. Our common goal in this life, once we see God, is to see him further and to possess him and desire him yet more. Contemplative prayer is an expression of this goal, albeit imperfectly, as far as we can achieve it in this life. The Holy Spirit begins the contemplative movement by putting into our hearts a gentle stirring of love. This love enables us to lift our hearts up to the Lord desiring him for his own sake and not for the sake of anything less. This desire is love reaching out for more love. God originates this love in us, God carries it out in us, and God is its goal through, in, and with us. We have no other goal or motive. There is no limit to this love. As St. Bernard says: the reason for love is love and the measure of love is measureless love.

If we could only be aware of God as God is constantly with us, we should be safe in mind and body and be assured of an overwhelming comfort. It is God's will that we should have this awareness even though we do not always recognize it. Even if we take the wings of the morning and settle at the furthest limits of the sea, even there his hand shall lead us and his right hand shall hold us fast (Psalm 139). We must believe and trust in him for he will be seen, he will be sought, he will be abided and he will be trusted.

Because it is the teaching of holy Church, we know by our faith that the Blessed Trinity made the human race in its own image and likeness. We also know by faith that when the human race, through Adam, fell so wretchedly by sin, this image and likeness was defaced. The only way we could be restored was by the same Trinity who created us. The Trinity created us because of his love and he would restore us by the same love. However, by that restoration, accomplished by Jesus our Savior, we are re-created to an even more perfect image of God than we had in our first creation. Oh happy fault of Adam that brought to us such a wonderful Savior!

God is greatly pleased by the soul that continues to seek him. Indeed, he is the ground of this seeking. The Holy Spirit enables us to seek, to suffer and to trust. When he wills and by his special grace, we are allowed to experience this love, even in this life, but in an imperfect manner. What pleases our Lord is that with faith, hope and love, we continue to seek him.

Understand this. Faith, hope and love are the means by which God communicates himself to us. We are given them to initiate our search for God. It is a loving search inspired by faith and hope. Thus to seek God is to find him by reason of that very seeking. Seeking is as good as finding and beholding. In this life it will be a darkened sight, occasionally illuminated by glimpses of spiritual light, until we are finally brought to see him in heaven even as we are seen.

The soul that clings to God with hope, either by seeking or beholding, gives him the greatest honor that is possible. Every soul is called and is given the grace to seek God. We should do this sincerely and with great care, without unreasonable stress or empty sorrow. We must also cling to God steadfastly for the sake of his love, without murmuring or opposing him. Believe in him, hope in him and love him. His working in us is secret yet he wishes it to be noticed, so he will give us sudden, brief glimpses of his blessed presence. Because of his graciousness and holy friendship, he desires that we trust in him. Praise him!

Possibly we have heard the words faith, hope and love so often that we have lost a real awareness of what they mean. These are called the theological virtues because they can only come from God, can only be sustained by God and have God as their object. Theology is the study of God so the theological virtues are virtues (powers) by which God communicates himself to us. They are the greatest gifts that even God could give us.

To have the theological virtues is to be the richest person in the world. Even God could not give us a greater gift. Just to desire these virtues is a blessing beyond compare. What could we desire that is greater than God? Who could we place our trust and hope in with greater confidence than in God. Who can we love but God in such a way as never to be disappointed and who can fulfill our deepest desires and satisfy our strongest and most fundamental longings.

If God is with us, it is through faith, hope and love. We cannot desire these virtues too much because to desire them is to desire God. Such a desire is itself God's gift and our very asking (praying) for these virtues is to receive them.

Pray then for faith. Pray for hope. Pray for love. Expect a response from God. No prayer is more pleasing to him. No other prayer has such absolute assurance of God's response. St. Thomas Aquinas tells us that the only prayer God must hear and respond to is the prayer for faith, hope and love. Other prayers he can only say "no" to, or delay an answer for our own good, or give us something greater. But to ask for the theological virtues is to ask for God. God desires this for us even more than we do for ourselves.

Chapter 5
God Is in All Things

From Shewings- Chapter 11

God is at the center of all his creation and in each smallest part of it. He is in all things. This is for us, a cause of uneasiness. If God is behind everything, large or small, then nothing is done by accident or ignorance. Rather, everything proceeds from the foreseeing wisdom of God. From all eternity his love and providence lead his creation to its perfect end which is his very self.

What then is evil? Because of their blindness and ignorance of the future, men and women experience things that seem to them to be risky and caused merely by chance and even by evil. But to the Lord, they are not so. Everything that he does is well done and he does everything. He is the center of all that is. All things begin from him, abide with him and find their completion in him.

It might well be that we are not given, in our time, a full understanding of the nature of sin and evil. We are called to contemplate the right-fullness of God's working. All that he does is correct and complete as he has determined from all eternity according to his divine, loving and perfect nature. Nothing that God has done or will do can ever lack its fullest completion according to his holy design. He is Father and has the power. He is Son and has the wisdom. He is the Holy Spirit and has the love which exercises that power and wisdom and manifests them in all creation. Indeed, he has the whole world in his hands.

Our Lord would have every man and woman truly understand that he and all his works are as good and perfect as they can possibly be. We do live in the most perfect of all worlds even though our ignorance does not always permit us to recognize it.

Before anything was made, God had already set all things in order, which order is perfect and shall never be changed. Everything was done out of the fullness of his goodness and the Trinity is pleased in all his works. In the end through his creation, God speaks to us: See! I am God; see! I am in all things; see! I do all things; see! My hands are never removed from my works; see! I lead all things to the end I ordered them to from all eternity. I do this by my power as the Father, by my wisdom as the Son and by my love as the Holy Spirit. How can anything be amiss? Thus are we led to understand that, together with Jesus, we are, in the graciousness of the Holy Spirit, the amen to the Father.

Our God is a personal God. He embraces all of his creation to the very limits of the cosmos. He is interested, concerned with and always aware of all that he has made even to dimensions of reality we are not aware of. Even so, his infinite care reaches out to the most galactic immensities. You and I exist somewhere in this vast panorama and we are loved, individually, personally, intimately and eternally.

Chapter 6
Wiel and Woe

From Shewings- Chapter 15

For everything there is a season, and a time for every matter under heaven: a time to be born and a time to die; a time to plant and a time to reap; a time to kill and a time to heal; a time to break down and a time to build up; a time to weep and a time to laugh; a time to mourn and a time to dance (Ecc. 2, 1- 4).

It is our personal experience that God gives us both well being and woe, pleasure and pain, first the one, then the other. Sometimes we are in such peace that it seems nothing on earth could ever disturb us. Then suddenly, we are left to our self in such weariness and pain that we scarcely have the patience to live. In this time of sorrow, we have no comfort but our faith, hope and love. In truth, we have these, but in feeling, we have them not.

Then our blessed Lord gives us again such comfort and rest in our soul that no sorrow or pain that might be suffered could possibly distress us. Then we are given again the heaviness and grief, then the joy and the pleasing, now the one and now the other. In the time of our joy, we say with St. Paul: Nothing shall separate me from the love of Christ. In the time of pain, we say with St. Peter: Lord, save me, I perish!

It is helpful for us to experience both this comfort and this desolation. God wants us to know that we are in his keeping in sorrow as well as in joy. For the profit of our soul, we are sometimes left to our self. Sin is not always the cause of our pain, nor is merit the cause of our joy. Our Lord suffers us to be in the one or the other as he wills. Both states are one love. Know this, however. It is God's will that we cling to the comfort with all our might. The pain is passing and shall be brought to naught. The bliss is intended to be everlasting. For this reason God does not will that we should follow the feelings of pain and sorrow but that we should suddenly pass over them and hold our self in endless joy and bliss in so far as we can.

So we should pray for relief in pain, sorrow and distress and look hopefully for healing and consolation from our Lord. At the same time, we carry our crosses knowing that they are permitted by a loving God and will lead us even as the cross led Jesus to the fullness of resurrected life.

Chapter 7
God's Plan

From Shewings- Chapter 18

At the last supper Jesus told us to perpetuate the memory of his suffering and death. Do this in memory of me. The mystery of his passion is not limited to Jerusalem of 2000 years ago. The pains and the death of Jesus are now hidden within the bonds of the powerful, wise and loving Trinity and he suffers and dies no more. Yet, what does it mean for us to remember it as he commands? The passion and death of Jesus is memorialized in everything that has its cause in him and in everyone who loves him.

Of those who love him, first place must be given to his mother, our Lady, St. Mary. Because of her love, both by nature as a mother and by grace as a handmaid of the Lord, a sword pierced her very soul. She was and will ever remain the one person most intimately united with our blessed Lord in his passion, death and resurrection.

After her, we enter into the great mystery of the Body of Christ. Those who love him the most are united with him the most in his passion even today. Who are they? They are those who most lovingly answer his call to take up their crosses daily and follow him. Of course, this would include St. John, the beloved disciple, the repentant St. Peter, the first martyr, St. Stephen, and all of the valiant witnesses of the early church. It also includes every soul that loves him throughout the entire history of the church until this very day, and even into the future, until the number of those who will be saved is complete. The passion of Christ is ever new, ever with us, ever living in his church and ever renewed in those who rejoice in their afflictions and make up in their own bodies what is lacking in the sufferings of Christ.

The passion of Christ also expresses itself in everything that owes its existence to God, the Son. Through him was made everything that was made. It is the good pleasure of God that he has set forth in Christ, as a plan for the fullness of time, to gather up all things in him, things in heaven and on earth. He has put all things under his feet, not only for this age, but for the ages to come and he has made him head over all things. All creation groans in travail, awaiting its redemption in Christ. He is the image of the invisible God, the firstborn of all creation, for in him all things in heaven and on earth were created: things visible and invisible, whether thrones or dominions, or rulers or powers -- all things have been created through him and for him. In him all things hold together. In him all the fullness of God was pleased to dwell and through him God was pleased to reconcile to himself all things, whether on earth or in heaven, by making peace through the blood of his cross. So the passion of Christ is real and active today in those who love him and in all his creation.

Chapter 8
Choose Jesus

From Shewings- Chapter 19

St. Therese tells us that the way to heaven is heaven. She is not offering us some naïve, unrealistic, superficial understanding of what she knows to be an arduous and narrow way. The Way of the Cross is the way to heaven. It is the Way of the Cross that is its self heaven. There is nothing that stands between the Cross and heaven. To look to the cross is to look to heaven.

St. Paul says (Romans 7) that nothing good dwells within me, that is, in my flesh. I can will what is right, but I cannot do it. For I do not do the good that I want, but the evil I do not want is what I do. Now if I do what I do not want, it is no longer I that do it, but sin that dwells within me. So I find it to be a law that when I want to do what is good, evil lies close at hand. For I delight in the law of God in my inmost self, but I see in my members another law at war with the law of my mind, making me captive to the law of sin that dwells in my members. Wretch that I am! Who will rescue me from this body of death? Thanks be to God through Jesus Christ our Lord. So then with my mind I am a slave to the law of God, but with my flesh I am a slave to the law of sin. The law of the Spirit of life in Christ Jesus has set me free from the law of death.

Our Lord, who willingly took the cross upon himself, also gives us our cross to bear willingly along with him. When we do this, we choose Jesus as our heaven at a time when choosing Jesus is to choose pain and suffering. Strangely enough, this should be a comfort to us that we are graced to choose Jesus to be our heaven at the time of his passion and sorrow. Thus we are given to learn that we must choose Jesus in woe if we would possess him forever in bliss.

There are times when we will repent of the love and generosity which prompted us to choose Jesus in his suffering. We seem then to be of two minds. One mind is inward and spiritual; the other is outward and based on our mortal fleshly weakness. It is this mortal fleshly weakness that turns us externally away from Jesus. This is the part of us that is master, which is united to Jesus. The external part does not draw the spiritual part to consent but, by grace, the spiritual part ultimately calls us to be one with Christ in bliss. The spiritual part is the internal peace and love which we still feel in spite of the weakness of the flesh. It is this part in which, with the power of the Father, the wisdom of the Son, and the steadfast love of the Holy Spirit, we choose Jesus to be our heaven.

Chapter 9
Sorrow into Joy

From Shewings- Chapters 20 to 21

Because Jesus, by reason of his union with the Trinity, is the noblest and highest human being, correspondingly, his suffering is the most intense and painful experience possible for a member of the human race. He that was the highest and worthiest was most fully made nothing. As much as he was the most sensitive and innocent, so much was he the strongest and mightiest to suffer. As long as Jesus was afflicted with the mortality of his human nature, he suffered and sorrowed for us. Yet now that he is risen and no longer mortal, he still suffers with us. He suffers for every man who sins and sorrows for every man's desolation. The love which he has for each soul is so strong that he is pleased to suffer for it in a degree surpassing all other suffering. The touch of grace allows us to see that the intensity of his pains shall be turned into a greater intensity of bliss by virtue of his passion. In a like manner for us, the heavier our burdens, the more joyful shall be our exultation.

If the Lord would allow us to experience his present blessed joy, there is no pain on earth that would concern us. Everything would be to us joy and bliss. Because he shows us now the time of his suffering as he bore it in this life and on the cross, we are in distress with him, as our present frailty demands. He allows this out of his goodness, so that for the little pain we suffer here, we shall have an exalted, eternal union with God which we could never have had otherwise. The harder our pains have been with him through his cross, the more shall our honor be with him in his kingdom.

God is not pleased with pain and suffering but he is pleased with our reaction to it. Our reaction, of course, must be to take up our crosses daily and follow Christ. In this way we are able to make up in our own bodies, as St. Paul says, what is lacking in the sufferings of Christ.

Our Lord redeemed the world through his suffering and death. He did not have to do it this way. The Father could have accepted a simple prayer from the lips of Jesus as sufficient to restore the world to his unsullied image and likeness. However, the great love the Son of God has for the human race compelled him to a redemptive death that witnessed to his conviction that greater love has no man than that he lays down his life for his friends.

Chapter 10
All Are Loved

From Shewings- Chapters 22 to 24

By reason of his mortal frailty, Jesus suffered and died for us so that we might know that greater love has no man than to lay down his life for his friends. His suffering was great but it was human. His love is infinitely greater because it is divine. What Jesus offers the human race in terms of his suffering and love, he offers to each individual man and woman ever to be created by God. Therefore, no one is without infinite value in the eyes of God. The unnamed millions of people who have come and gone on this earth since the beginning of creation are known, each one by his name, to our loving God. The millions upon millions who have been killed by wars, stricken by plagues, destroyed by natural disasters and buried in mass graves, or not buried at all, are individually known and loved by him as his own sons and daughters. Jesus gladly died for each one of us and rose that we might join him in his joy and bliss. Our Lord would have us know that it is a joy, a bliss and an endless satisfaction to him that he suffered his passion and rose from the dead for us.

It is through Jesus Christ that we are given to know the working of the Trinity in our salvation. He who sees Jesus sees the Father. Whoever loves him will be loved by the Father. In Jesus and in all the deeds he has done for our salvation is the Father well pleased. This pleasing of the Father is the greatest gift Jesus could possibly receive. Thus we are not only his by our redemption but also by the gracious gift of the Father. All this is done in love through the working of the Holy Spirit.

We are Jesus' joy, his reward and his honor. So precious are we to Jesus that he sees as nothing all his travail, his passion and his cruel and shameful death. If it were possible, he would die again for each one of us and it would seem to him as nothing, for the sake of his love. The human frailty of Christ may suffer only once but his goodness never ceases to offer that suffering for us out of his love. (What confidence this should give us in our prayers. If Jesus gladly gives us his all without our asking, how readily would he not give us lesser things in response to our urgent prayers?)

As far as the heavens are above the earth, so far does his love surpass all his pains. His passion was a noble, honorable deed done in time by the working of love. But this love was without beginning, is now, and ever shall be without ending. Thus all this wonderful work of our salvation was planned by the Trinity in perfection from all time. In it the Father is well pleased, and gives the fullness of bliss to his Son in the gracious love of the Holy Spirit.

Through the passion of Christ, the Trinity has joy and bliss and endless satisfaction. For joy, we understand the pleasure of the Father, for bliss, we see the honor of the Son, and for endless satisfaction, we recognize the Holy Spirit. The Father is pleased, the Son is honored and the Holy Spirit is satisfied.

God wills that we take heed to the bliss that is in the blessed Trinity because of our salvation and that our own joy should do likewise. God wants us to be strengthened and comforted and that our soul be occupied merrily with the grace of our salvation. We are his bliss and he takes joy in us as we shall in him forever.

We are told by theologians that the most sublime doctrine from divine revelation is the doctrine of the Triune God. How God can be one in three or three in one has been the subject of theological speculation since the first century. Wars have been fought, nations have risen and fallen, and people have been burned at the stake, imprisoned, tortured and exiled because of theological disagreements about the tri-unity of God. This cannot be pleasing to God.

Too often the Trinity has been treated as a theological abstraction with little or no practical involvement in the reality of the church and the lives of individual Christians. It has been present only as some kind of intellectual conundrum in the minds of theological speculators. Dame Julian would have us understand the Trinity as personal, real, loving, intimate and living in our hearts. The Trinity embodies for us the functions and concerns that we experience in all of our human relationships. God is father and mother, son and brother, daughter and spouse. All of the wonderful and loving offices performed in all of our human relations with one another are but vague reflections of the power, wisdom and love of the Father, Son and Holy Spirit.

Chapter 11
Joy in His Mother

From Shewings- Chapter 25

It is the blessed will of our Lord Jesus that we consider his mother, our Lady St. Mary. We consider her as she was with child, as she was before the cross and as she is now in glory. After himself, she is the highest joy that he might reveal to us. She is the most noble of all his creatures and gives to him the greatest pleasure and honor. He wants us to see in her how much we are loved. He wants us to rejoice in him in the love he has for her and in her love for him. Our Lord speaks to all mankind as though to one person and wishes us to know that it was for love of us that he made her so noble and worthy. This pleases him and he wills that it pleases us also. Jesus teaches us to appreciate the beauty of her blessed soul, her truth, wisdom and love, so that we may see in her a model for ourselves. As we find our joy in him, so he wants us to take pleasure in his mother.

It is in the prayer of Mary in response to the angel Gabriel's visit that we see the working of God and the model for our own response to God's mercy and grace. Her soul magnifies the Lord because he has had regard for her humility. Our Lady knew who she was. She knew her nothingness without God. She was nothing, she had nothing, and she desired nothing except the love of God.

These are the precise conditions under which God gives himself to us. The virtue of humility, that is, our awareness of our own nothingness, impels us to turn to God. It brings out in us a deep, interior desire for God which is always present at the still point at the center of our being but which is often hidden or even buried by our false self. Only when this is freed by letting go does God who is mighty do great things in, with, and for us.

The proud can never experience this. They depend upon their own resources. This is a deceptive way of seeing themselves as God, thinking they are in control of their own destiny. This is what they will get – control of their own destiny – which can only lead to nothingness. With God's mercy and grace, through humility and love, we can gradually let go of our deceptions, turn to God and find our fulfillment in him. This will take place, if we only desire it, by the power of

the Father, the wisdom of the Son and the goodness of the Holy Spirit.

Chapter 12
Rest in the Lord

From Shewings- Chapter 26

Our souls shall never have rest until they come to the Lord, knowing him as the fullness of our joy and of life itself. This is why he took upon himself the very name which God revealed to Moses, I Am! He said: I am the way, the life, the truth, I am the good Shepherd, I am the vine, and I am the door of the sheepfold. I am that which is highest, that which you love and enjoy. I am that which you serve, which you long for, which you desire. I am that which is all and which holy Church preaches and teaches to you.

That which he reveals to us is his very self and this revelation surpasses all our knowledge and understanding. It is not really possible to put into words the joy that our Lord is to and for us. He is more than our minds can comprehend, our hearts can wish for and our souls can desire. The grace of God must give to every man to know, to love and to receive the truth which he is.

Again and again we are reminded of St. Augustine's prayer, "Our hearts are made for you, O Lord, and they cannot rest until they rest in you". In the language of today, the opposite of the word "rest" is "burn out". It means that due to our hyperactivity we have exhausted, burned out, all of our personal strengths and resources. This happens even to good people who are trying to serve the Body of Christ in strong social activity. Too often they neglect their prayer life, draw upon their own personal strength and resources. Before long they are exhausted, emotionally, spiritually and physically. The needs of these people are overwhelming and they see their inability to make any real changes for the good. They neglect to allow their hearts to rest in the Lord in prayer, to receive the spiritual nourishment the Holy Spirit offers. The result is burn out. The solution is realizing the need and making the time to rest in the Lord.

Burn out should be seen as a way the Lord brings us to a personal experience of our nothingness. It should be seen then as God's call. "Come to me all you who labor and are heavy burdened, and I will give you rest!"

Chapter 13
Why Is There Sin?

From Shewings- Chapter 27

Nothing but sin hinders us from the Lord whom we desire. Were it not for sin, we should all have been clean and unsullied in the image and likeness of God in which we were created. Why then did the great foreseeing wisdom of God permit sin in the first place? Then all would have been well. Jesus responds to this question by assuring us that, in fact, sin is necessary and yet all shall be well and all manner of things shall be well.

By the word, sin, let us understand all that is not good: all the humiliations of Christ's passion, together with all the pains and sufferings, spiritually and physically, of all his creatures. For we shall all be humbled following our master, Jesus, until we are purified from the evils inherent in our mortal flesh and in all worldly affections. Thus sin embraces all the pains that ever were or ever shall be, including especially, the sufferings of Christ, which were the greatest of all.

Sin, which has no substance in itself, is known by the pain it causes. This pain does have substance because it humbles and purifies us, gives us true self-knowledge and makes us turn to God for mercy. The will of God, which especially includes the passion of Christ, is a comfort to us against all this darkness. Jesus is near and walking on the water.

Our Lord rejoices in our tribulations with the same joy he had when he suffered his passion for us. He allows each of his beloved friends their own crosses whereby they are blamed and despised in this world. He does this, not because he blames them, but because he has pity and compassion. He wishes to prevent the harm that we should otherwise take from the pomp and vainglory the world offers us. When the truth of our feeble nature allows us to be aware of our vain affections and vicious pride, he shall gather us up, meek, mild, clean and holy into union with him. Each kind, compassionate affection that we lovingly feel for one another is this joy of our Lord working in us.

Our Lord wants us to rejoice in the bliss he gives us in all the good things of our life. He also wants us to be comforted in our pain by understanding that it will, by virtue of his passion, all be turned to our honor and gain. We will see that we do not suffer alone but with him, the very ground of our being, whose sufferings so far surpass anything we may be burdened with that we cannot even imagine it. When we see that our sins deserve pain yet his love excuses us from it, we will be preserved from murmuring and despair. We will see that he does away with all our blame and mercifully looks upon us as innocent and beloved children. We are his beloved children in whom he is well pleased.

Chapter 14
Two Levels of Truth

From Shewings- Chapters 29 to 31

O f all the evils that have afflicted the human race, the greatest is the sin of Adam. Every evil, sin, affliction, harm or woe, ever to occur subsequently, has followed from that original sin. It would be blind and totally insensitive of us to ignore the human calamities that we experience. And yet God reveals to us that his love is unconditional and we live in the most perfect of all possible worlds.

Somehow we are called to believe in the face of all odds that all shall be well. How can this be? We are also called to believe that Jesus made complete and perfect satisfaction and amends to our Father in heaven for Adam's sin. But if Jesus satisfied completely for Adam's sin, the greatest sin of all, then he must also have satisfied for every lesser evil that followed from that sin. This atonement gives God more honor and is more pleasing to him than ever did the dishonor or the harm of Adam's sin. Oh happy sin of Adam that gave to us so wonderful a Savior! He has made well what was the most evil and thereby gives us to know that he shall also make well every lesser sin and evil.

The Lord wants us to understand that his truth is revealed in two levels. The first level concerns our Savior and our salvation. It is open, fair, clear and lucid. All men and women who are or who will be of good will are included in this level. Until now we are obligated to God, and the Holy Spirit calls, counsels and teaches us, in a personal, spiritual manner in our hearts. He also teaches us outwardly and objectively through the doctrines of the church. He does both by the same grace. Our Lord wills that we be fully occupied on this level, rejoicing in him, as he rejoices in us. The more completely that we give ourselves to this truth, with humility and reverence, the more pleased he is with us and the more profit it is to us in our joy.

The second level of truth includes everything not related to our personal salvation. This level is closed to us and secret because it belongs to the Lord's hidden plan not yet revealed to us. It is proper to God to have his hidden plan in peace and it is proper to us, his servants, out of respect and obedience, not to know it in its entirety. The

Lord looks with compassion on our anxiety to know everything but it pleases him when we are satisfied to know and to do only his will. We are then united with the saints in heaven whose desire is ruled after the will of God. They desire nothing but God's will, as should we. This teaches us to trust in our Savior alone for everything.

Nevertheless, the Lord does answer all of our questions and doubts from the unity of his Trinity. He says: I may make all things well. We are to understand this as coming from the Father who has the power to do it. He says: I can make all things well. We are to understand this as coming from the Son who has the wisdom to do so. He says: I will make all things well, as coming from the Holy Spirit who has the goodness and love actually to put into effect the power of the Father and the wisdom of the Son to make all things well. Herein are three persons and one truth! Finally, our Lord touches upon his hidden plan and promises that we shall see for ourselves that all manner of things shall be well.

We see in the Book of Hebrews that God had a hidden plan, a mystery in the Old Testament. Jesus, the Messiah, the Son of God, the incarnate Wisdom of the Father is hidden in every passage of the Hebrew Scriptures. It is only in these latter days that this mystery has been revealed to us by the Holy Spirit.

There are more mysteries yet to be revealed. No one knows the times or the particulars, not even the Son of Man. The Holy Spirit continues to guide the Body of Christ towards the ultimate fulfillment of its union with God. This involves suffering, crosses, consolations and hidden mysteries. God has the whole church and each individual in his hands and all manner of things will be well.

Chapter 15
The Great Deed

From Shewings- Chapters 31 to 32

On the cross, Jesus said: I thirst. He was speaking of both a physical and a spiritual need. As man, his body demanded water, as God, his thirst is the longing of his divine love for each of Adam's children who had become his brothers and sisters by his incarnation. This thirst will last until the last man and woman is saved. His thirst is his desire to have the entire human race one with him in a unity surpassing our present oneness. He has pity and compassion for us and desires that we be one with him. His wisdom and his love will allow this fullness of unity to come at the best possible time which only he knows.

Dame Julian teaches an extraordinary understanding she received in her visions. Two things which the Lord spoke to her heart were the foundations for it. He told her that all things shall be well and that she shall see for herself that all manner of things shall be well. The first understanding is that God wants us to know that he takes heed not only to noble and great things, but also to low and simple things. Even the least thing shall not be forgotten. Indeed, the tiniest sparrow that falls from the sky does not escape his all seeing eyes and his provident care. All manner of things shall be well.

The second understanding God wants us to have, follows from this. We see and experience, in our own lives and in the lives of others, deeds so evil and harmful that it does not seem possible that they should ever end well. So we look upon these deeds in sorrow, not realizing how lovingly God sees them. We do this because of our ignorance of the power, wisdom and love of the Trinity. When God says: you shall see for yourself, it is as if he is telling us that we should take heed to what he is telling us right now in faith and trust and, at the end, we will truly see it in the fullness of joy. By these words God intends to comfort us greatly with regard to all his future works in our behalf.

Julian says, "There is a Deed which the Blessed Trinity shall do in the last day, as I understand it. And exactly when and how this deed shall be done is known only to Christ." The Holy Spirit, in his goodness and love, wants us to know that this will happen. The might of the Father and the wisdom of the Son, out of the same love, will conceal from us what it shall be and how it shall be done.

The Lord wants us to know that this Deed shall be done to set our souls at peace in love. It allows us to let go of the troublesome things that might hinder us from truly enjoying him. Just as the Blessed Trinity made all things out of nothing, so the same Trinity shall make well all that is not well. How it shall be done, no creature beneath Christ knows it, nor shall know it, until it is done.

Julian wondered greatly at all this when she considered the teaching of the church that God's Word is true and to be trusted. But God's Word, through the Church's teaching, tells us that many creatures shall be condemned: the Angels that fell into pride, men who die without baptism, or in heresy, or in mortal sin. How then is it possible that all things shall be well as the Lord taught her?

The Lord answered this by telling Julian that that which is impossible to her is not impossible to him. His word in the Church and in Julian's heart will both be kept. She should hold fast to her faith in the Church's teaching and also in the Lord's promise that all things shall be well. This great Deed that our Lord shall do will save his word and he shall make all things well that are not well.

Chapter 16
The Token of Sin

From Shewings- Chapters 38 to 39

Every soul that comes to heaven is so precious to God that his goodness actually rewards it for its sins or rewards it for its response to sin, namely; repentance. In heaven, one's sins shall not be a cause of shame but of honor. In truth, every sin that we commit in this life causes us pain. But in heaven that same sinful soul, because of God's love, is given a great joy. Just as on Earth, different sins are punished with diverse pains according to their severity, so in heaven they are accordingly rewarded with diverse joys precisely in relation to the pains they brought about on Earth.

There are many happy examples of this both in the Old Testament and in the New. David sinned grievously. He has been blessed greatly. Mary Magdalene, St. Peter and St. Paul, and numerous more recent saints, known by the church to have sinned, are in heaven not shamed but honored. They have sinned greatly but have loved even more greatly. In heaven the token of sin is turned to honor.

God has suffered many saints to fall while still mercifully preserving them from condemnation. Because of their contrition and humility, God has given them in heaven greater joys than they would have had if they had never sinned. They had sinned much but they do love more even because of their sins. All this is to make us glad and merry in love!

It is a sign of his holy friendship that our Lord protects us so lovingly when we are in sin. He secretly touches our soul and shows us our sin by the precious light of his mercy and grace. As a result, we are able to see our own foulness which, in turn, makes us think that God is angry with us. This is humility and the fear of the Lord. Then the Holy Spirit stirs up in us contrition and prayer and a desire to make amends to appease God and find rest for our souls. We are then graced with a sure hope that God has forgiven us our sins. Led by the Spirit we turn to the church for the sacraments and we humbly and obediently receive our penance and absolution if need be. This meekness pleases the Lord.

At this time, we may even be visited with crosses from the world, the flesh, and the devil.

We may feel that the Lord has deserted us and that we have deserved it. This is the humility that our Lord looks for and, because of it; he raises us up high by his grace. We are given great contrition for our sins, compassion for others, and true longing for God.

By contrition we are cleansed, by compassion we are prepared, and by true longing for God we are made worthy. All souls that have been sinners on Earth are brought to heaven by these three means. They are the medicines by which our souls are healed. Even though our souls are healed, our wounds are still seen by God, not as marks of shame but of honor. His love assigns no blame.

The Lord wants us to know that we should never despair even for frequent or mortal sins. Our failures do not interfere with his love. We are to realize that while we may not always feel his peace and love, they are still with us. Actually by our falling, we give the Lord further occasion to defend us. The greater our need and the danger we are in, the greater is his protection for us. God and his love are the ground of our life and being.

The pain resulting from sin, God turns into

happiness. The sorrow resulting from our awareness of our sinfulness, God turns into joy. God
has compassion and pity for us in our weaknesses.
Neither blame nor condemnation comes from
God. He is a lover, not a judge.

God sees our world, not as someone separated
and apart from it, but, as it were, from within.
He is intrinsic to his creation and especially to
humankind. All that is is sustained in existence
by God. His love, wisdom and goodness creates,
guides and directs everything and everyone.
God is intrinsic to us especially by reason of the
Incarnation. He became one of us that we might
become one with him. He is the ground of our
life and being.

The poet, Gerard Manly Hopkins, expresses
this beautifully when he wrote: the world is
charged with the grandeur of God even though
man has soiled and spoiled it, the world is always
on the brink of a new dawn. The theological virtue
of hope is one of the three ways by which God
communicates himself to us. This is not something he is going to do, he is always doing it. He
is the promise and the fulfillment of the promise.
He is the not-yet and the already-here. The vic-
tory has been won for us, we have only to reach

out and claim it.

Chapter 17
True Prayer

From Shewings- Chapter 40

O
ur gracious Lord shows himself to the soul with glad cheer and friendly welcoming. Knowing that the soul had been imprisoned in pain, he says: My beloved, I have been with you during all your sorrow and now you can see my love and our union in joy. It is the graceful working of the Holy Spirit and the power of Christ's passion that brings us from sin to mercy and grace. Even on Earth, when we turn to God, we are received in honor and joy just as we will be received in heaven. As St. Paul tells us, "It is God who is at work in you, both to will and to work for his good pleasure (Philippians 2)."

All manner of things are made ready for us by the great goodness of God. At times we will feel peace and love even if not in its fullness. God longs to give us this fullness of joy which will come as we pray and long for our Lord, Jesus Christ.

We must beware here of the danger of presumption. The spiritual comfort we receive from repenting our sins may tempt us to think that our sins are actually good. After all, it is because of them that we are rewarded with God's forgiveness and compassion. Beware of this! It is untrue. Love makes us hate sin. A well disposed soul, seeing the great love of God, will hate and be ashamed of his sins. He will realize that sin is vile and to be hated more than any pain on Earth or in hell. Indeed, for such a soul, there is no hell but sin

No matter how great our sins may be, when we give ourselves to humility and charity, we are made beautiful and stainless by the working of mercy and grace. The Trinity has the power, wisdom, and desire to bring us to salvation. Christ himself is the ground of all the moral laws governing the lives of Christians. He wills that we love the sinner but hate the sin. Even as he loved us and died for us while we were yet sinners, so he bids us to love ourselves and our fellow Christians in like manner. Thus we shall hate sin as God hates it and love the sinner as God loves him. This should be for us, a source of endless comfort and security.

Actually we should not be concerned about our particular sins, that is, by sins we have committed in the past. These we have confessed before the Lord, especially in the sacrament of reconciliation. There is no point dwelling on these sins or even thinking about them. What is the point? They are forgiven, we are reconciled.

What we should be concerned about is our sinfulness. By this is meant our awareness of our false-self and our prideful tendency to prefer our own wills to that of God. Our sins are forgiven but we must always be mindful of our sinfulness.

Chapter 18
The Ground of Our Prayer

From Shewings- Chapters 41 to 42

At times we feel as barren after our prayers as we were before. This is foolishness and is caused by our feebleness. We lack trust and think that God does not hear us because of our unworthiness and lack of faith. This is not true. If we lacked faith, we would not pray at all. All we need is faith the size of a mustard seed. Because of our many needs, real and imaginary, the prayers of petition are often on our lips and in our hearts. The Lord would have us know that we do not ask him for anything that is good without being first empowered by his grace. He is actually the foundation, the ground of our beseeching. It is his pleasure to answer our prayers because he is the source of them in the first place. The most important thing we can ask of God is his mercy and grace. It is impossible that we should ask for this and not receive it. Our asking is not the cause of God's goodness to us. Rather God's goodness is the cause of our asking -- and receiving.

Asking good things from God, either for ourselves or for others comes to us through the grace of the Holy Spirit. He unites and fastens our will to God's will. Our Lord makes himself to be like us by taking on our human nature. He becomes human and we become divine. His will is ours and our will is his. His prayer is ours and our prayer is his. How could he not take pleasure in our askings? He wants us to pray from our hearts even when our prayers seem to be dry and barren, weak, and feeble and, above all, unanswered. Every prayer is made with God-given faith or it could not be made at all. But faith is the substance of the things that appear not. We do not grasp the substance of our prayers being answered but faith assures us it will be.

Because God knows and is pleased with the answers that he will give to our prayer, he wants us to pray continuously in his sight. God accepts our goodwill and our labor, as weak as it may be, in spite of our feelings that he is absent and ignoring us. So we must work at our praying and work at our efforts to live a Christian life, knowing we have his help and his grace. He is the ground of our beseeching and he is its reward.

Prayer is more than asking for things. It is also thanking God. We thank him even while we are asking, with the full assurance of his loving reply. God's grace stirs up this thanksgiving. Sometimes, it is just an inward act making us love God and thanking him with a quiet joy. At other times, it might break out in joyful words of praise. Sometimes, when our heart is dry and without feeling, our reason, aided by grace, speaks to us with a clear understanding. We are graced to remember what our Lord suffered to prove his love and show his great goodness. Then the power of the Lord touches our soul and gives life to our heart. Then by his grace, we pray with joy. This in itself is a blessed prayer of thanksgiving.

Chapter 19
Prayer and Trust

From Shewings- Chapter 42

To understand prayer, we must realize that God is its real source and that it comes from his goodness. The bottom line of our prayer is that our will shall be turned into his will. As Jesus prayed in the garden: Not my will but thine. The ultimate fruit and goal of all our prayer is union with God in all things. Thy will be done on earth as it is in heaven. And we will make it so because he will help us.

Our prayer must be informed and filled with a firm belief in the power and reliability of God, if we are to honor the Lord as he deserves. To do otherwise is to bring unnecessary pain upon ourselves. To have trust in our prayer, we do not always have to feel it. We simply must know and desire it. This will bring us to an awareness that God is the ground of our beseeching and it is given to us by his love. No one can ask his grace and mercy in true prayer unless it first be given to him.

It happens to all of us at times that we pray earnestly for a long time and yet think that we have not been heard or answered. This should not grieve us or discourage us. It is the Lord's way of telling us that the time is not yet ripe. There will be a better time, a greater gift, and further grace if we try to wait patiently and continue our prayer.

God wants us to realize that he is All in All. He wants our hearts and our minds to be grounded with all our might in him. This is how we are to abide in him, take our rightful place with him, and see that he is truly the light of the world and our own personal light.

There are three things that we should understand for our comfort in prayer. The first is our noble creation in the image of God. The second is our precious re-creation through our redemption in Christ. The third is that God has put all things under our feet for our service and well-being. He has done all of this for us before we were even able to send forth the weakest of prayers -- before we even existed. His greatest deeds are already done! Realizing this with thanks and praise, we should pray for the deed God is now doing for us. He is ruling and guiding us in this life for his greater honor and glory, to bring us to eternal happiness.

Thus he has done everything that even he can do.

To all these wonderful works of God, we should have two responses. We should realize that he has done them and that we should respond to them in prayer. If we pray but do not realize what he has already done, we are apt to be sad, doubtful, and burdened. That is not to his honor. Also, if we realize what he has done, but do not pray, we fail in our duty to God and in the debt of thanks we owe him. So we must do both; see his grace and mercy already in our lives, and respond to it with trust, praise and love. To recognize what God does and to pray as a result of it, is to his honor and to our earthly and eternal welfare.

Chapter 20
Contemplative Prayer

From Shewings- Chapter 43

Prayer unites the soul to God. Because of our redemption, the soul is always united to God but by sin, it is often seemingly in a condition quite apart from him. Then prayer becomes for us a witness and a confirmation that we are conforming our will to his. Thus we appease our conscience and dispose ourselves further to grace. God wants us to pray, he teaches us to pray, and he enables us to pray. He looks on us with love and stirs us to pray for those very gifts that are his pleasure to bestow on us. He gives us the gift of prayer and goodwill and promises us an eternal reward.

In our prayer God hears us beseeching him to accomplish his will in and for us -- the very thing he desires to do. God is so pleased with this, that he responds as though he were actually in our debt, even though every good deed that we do is, in fact, done by him.

Sometimes the Lord shows himself to the soul

and we have that which we desire; an immediate experience of God, albeit, in a manner darkly. In this life no man may see God and live. That is reserved for heaven when we shall see even as we are seen. However, even in this life, we can have an obscure vision of God in contemplation. This is somewhat like the experience of Moses on Mount Sinai who hid in the cleft of the rock and saw God pass by but only, as it were, in his hindermost parts. In this prayer, the Holy Spirit puts into our heart a gentle stirring of love by which we are able to lift our heart to God, as it were, without intermediaries, desiring him for his own sake and not for his gifts. During this time, we cease to pray with our intelligence but only with our loving wills. We ask for nothing because we have all! Our physical senses are quieted and we await the fullness of our spiritual senses to be touched by the finger of God, to truly see and hear and feel him spiritually, to breathe in his spirit and taste and see that the Lord is good.

This is a high prayer that goes beyond our understanding. We are one with God to whom we pray, seeing him and still desiring him further even as, in a greater and more lucid manner, we shall do in heaven. This is a prayer of faith and love, together with affection and spiritual feeling.

At other times, when we do not experience God in this contemplative manner, we feel the need to pray with thoughts and words. We feel the need to pray this way because we feel troubled and restless and left to ourselves. We do not experience our union with the Lord as formerly. God permits this in order to make our soul supple and pliant while giving us a deep knowledge of ourselves, which is humility and which is necessary for a deeper knowledge of God. Yet he still loves us as much, or even more, than we had experienced in our contemplation. So when we recognize our need for God, we pray. Then our good Lord comes to us, giving us the longing for him we seek. He, as it were, follows us wherever we go, giving us that special, contemplative grace to be united to him directly in love without the intermediaries of words or thoughts. Then we follow him as he draws us to him by love. His marvelous goodness surpasses and fulfills all our powers and he works in us all manner of things with his Trinitarian power, wisdom, and goodness. He goes beyond all our imagining and our thoughts. We can then do nothing but behold him (darkly) and enjoy him with a great desire to be completely united to him, to be centered in him, and to delight in his goodness. So it is, even in this life. What shall it be in the next?

The man who desires God is the richest man on earth. When the psalmist asks: What do I have in heaven but you oh God? He is acknowledging this: What else is there to have? When we have God, we have everything. To desire God is to have God because that very desire is already the answer to our longing. Desire is the child of love. It is itself love.

To love God is to be bonded with him, to be as Dame Julian says, oned with God. This bond of love is not a complacent stability but a vibrant, lively eagerness for even more love, ever reaching forward, surging ahead, ever satisfied but ever longing for more.

Chapter 21
Truth, Wisdom and Love

From Shewings- Chapter 44

The fullness of God's will is accomplished in every man, in all that God does. Truth comes from the Father and Wisdom from the Son. Truth sees God and Wisdom beholds God and from these two comes that holy delight in God which is Love. Where there is Truth and Wisdom there is Love. God is eternal, uncreated Truth, Wisdom and Love. Man's soul, although it is created, has these same Trinitarian properties. It sees God in truth. It knows God in wisdom, and it enjoys God in love. So in a marvelous way, God enjoys man and man enjoys God. And so, in awe and wonder, man sees his God and Creator, so high and great and good that he seems himself as nothing in comparison. This is true humility. The clarity of this truth and wisdom makes man see and understand that he was created for love and that everything else was created to make love possible.

Eventually man will not see himself as nothing because he will not see himself at all. He will, when God so touches his soul, be annihilated as

Margarete Parete insists. He will be like a drop of water in the ocean. He will become a naked intent towards God, not <u>somebody</u> who is a naked intent but just a towardness even as the Word is a towardness to the Father. He will even be able to go one step further than St. Paul who said, "I live now not I but Christ lives in me". Rather he will say, "I live now not I but Christ lives". There will be no I and Thou because we will be so oned with God as to become God. The Church Father did not hesitate to say that we will be divinized. What God is by nature, we shall become by grace. The simple desire God put into our hearts by the Spirit of Christ at the onset of our spiritual journey somehow contains in seed the fullness of that desire. One with God!

God is also truth. As we image God, truth must also be in us. You shall know the truth and the truth shall set you free. Free from what? Free from all that is not God, from all that is false in us, and from our false selves. In the degree that we do not realize the truth about ourselves, we live a lie. We are liars. The devil is the prince of lies. We either belong to him or we seek the truth and belong to the Lord. He who is not with Him is against Him. Knowing the truth about ourselves is to know what we are without God – nothing!

But full humility is the full truth, that is, knowing what we are with God. In this way are the lowly exalted.

Chapter 22
Two Judgments

From Shewings- Chapter 45

Man has a higher nature and a lower. His higher nature is not a separately existing component of his being but rather is the idea of man which has existed from all eternity in the mind and heart of God. Because of God's righteousness, this higher nature is protected in its image and likeness of God for all eternity, safe and sound. He chose us in Christ before the foundation of the world to be holy and blameless before him in love. Man has also a lower, sense nature since the time of his actual creation on this earth. This lower nature is changeable, now one thing, now another, according as it relates to its higher nature in God. This higher nature is inward and spiritual and hidden in God, while the lower nature is visible, outward and sensible. Because of this diversity, man's wisdom and judgment is sometimes good and easy, and sometimes hard and grievous.

When man's awareness of his lower nature is easy and good, it is so inasmuch as it belongs to the righteousness of God and partakes, as it were, of the higher nature. When his lower nature is hard and grievous, it is because of sin. When this is so, the good Lord restores it by his mercy and grace, merited by his passion, and so brings it to righteousness.

Self-knowledge, humility, is foundational for knowledge of God. In this life, our lower or sense nature cannot fully know its true self. It comes only gradually to know the truth about itself by virtue of its conformity with its higher nature. It is only after death that we will fully know ourselves. Only at this point, will we fully know God according to our capacity.

Meanwhile, from our personal, earthly point of view, we need to know that we are sinners. We do those things we should not do and we leave undone, deeds we ought to do. Our experience and our judgment tells us we are worthy of God's wrath. At the same time, we are given by his mercy and grace to know that he is God, and Life, Truth and Love. He knows no wrath nor ever shall. Anger is contrary to his Trinitarian power, wisdom and love. God is all goodness and in his goodness, there is no place for wrath. Because there is no place for wrath, there is no place or need for forgiveness in his sight. Our soul is so united to God in that goodness that there is nothing between God and our soul except love.

Chapter 23
Mercy and Grace

From Shewings- Chapters 47 to 49

W e know that we often fail to give our attention to God. Instead, we replace him by looking toward ourselves. Instead of focusing on his might, wisdom and goodness, we give ourselves over to our own sins and sinfulness. The feeling of our sins is one of travail and turbulence and all manner of pain, both spiritual and physical. In gracious response to this condition, the Holy Spirit, who is the endless life of our soul, keeps us secure by his grace and works in us peace and comfort. He redirects the soul toward God and makes it docile.

The only anger there is, is on man's part and God forgives us for this. Anger is an aggressive opponent of peace and love. It comes from a failing of might, wisdom or goodness. It mars our image and likeness of God. Obviously then, it is not from God or to be found in God. It is only in us. By reason of our sins and sinfulness, we are in a constant state of opposition to peace and love.

The source and ground of God's mercy is his love and goodness. The work of his mercy is keeping us in that love. Mercy is God's gracious working in love together with his compassion. It is his mercy which, because it is his love, makes all things work together unto good. By his mercy and love, God suffers us to fail to a certain degree. Inasmuch as we fail, to that degree, we fall. Inasmuch as we fall, to that degree, we die. We die because we fail to see and feel our very life which is God. Our failing is dreadful, our falling is shameful and our dying is sorrowful. But in all this, God's sweet eye of pity and love is never taken from us, nor does the working of his mercy ever cease.

God's mercy and grace work together in God's love. Mercy is a compassionate way of working that belongs to the tender, loving motherhood of God. Grace is an honor bestowing way of working that belongs to his fatherhood and his Lordship both in the one, divine love. Mercy works by nurturing, preserving, patiently enduring, giving life and healing, and all this, with a tender maternal love. Grace works by raising up, rewarding, constantly surpassing whatever our desires and our labor deserves, revealing the greatness of God's royal Lordship and fatherhood. This too is from the abundance of his love and goodness. This grace is what turns our dreadful failing into endless consolation, our shameful falling into an honorable rising and our sorrowful dying into a holy, blessed life.

Our opposition to God here on earth brings us pain, shame and sorrow. Heavenly grace, however, brings us comfort, honor, joy and more. The day will come when we will thank and bless the Lord for the sorrows he allowed us. We will realize that they have brought us greater fruits of his love then we could have received in any other way. It is important to understand that God's mercy and forgiveness slackens our anger and brings us peace, both with him and in ourselves. In God there is no anger hence there is no need for forgiveness. Everything in our life is grounded and rooted in love. Without love there is no life.

The grace-filled soul sees far into the marvelous goodness of God and sees that we are endlessly united to him in love. Truly it is impossible for him to be at the same time angry and friendly. They are contraries. This would be a house divided against itself. God takes away our personal wrath and replaces it with humility and peace. He is ever united to us in a meek and gentle love. How could he then be angry? Where the Lord is present, there is peace. There is no manner of anger in God. If he were angry, even for an instant, we would cease to exist. We receive our existence from the endless power of the Father, the endless wisdom of the Son and the endless goodness of the Holy Spirit. So too, are we preserved in existence by the same Trinity.

We often feel in ourselves wretchedness, strife and confusion. But, at the same time, we are in every way enclosed and wrapped in the gentleness, goodness and graciousness of God. It is this endless friendship which gives us our place, our life and our being in God. That same goodness which saves us from perishing when we are in sin constantly gives us peace. Through this goodness, we are brought to see the real truth about ourselves. This truth, which is the virtue of humility, brings us to a fear of God which, in turn, reveals to us our need for him. Thus we are led to find our sufficiency in Christ. Truly when we are weak, then we are strong. Our blindness and frailty causes tribulation, distress and woe, yet we are securely safe by the merciful protection of God that we may not perish. In his goodness the Lord does not permit our unrest and sorrow to destroy us. He is our very peace and our loving protector.

The journey toward God is a journey of love. Because God is love, the journey begins with him. Love starts its journey with God, comes down from heaven and then proceeds to return to heaven. So it begins, is carried out, and concludes by, in and with God. Is it any wonder that for those who love God, all things work together unto good? Love then must govern everything that we think, say or do. Our relationships must be manifestations of our love. We must love one another as Jesus loves us. Love your neighbor for the love of God.

Love is not discouraged. Even when we fail in love, that very love will inspire us to start over again. God's love for us is never ending. Even sin does not extinguish it. We too must never allow our sins to extinguish our love but must make all the more effort to love because of them.

Chapter 24
Bipolar Spirituality

From Shewings- Chapter 50

God is all about relationships. The oneness of the Trinity is an eternal, unsurpassable unity of three persons. The Trinity's internal relationships which are the Father, the Son and the Holy Spirit are expressed in creation and especially in the highest form of physical creation, the human race. The heart of God rejoices in his relationships with us.

There are five special relationships in which God rejoices. God rejoices because he is our father and our mother and our soul is his child. He rejoices that he is our spouse and that our soul is his beloved wife. Christ rejoices that he is our brother and Jesus rejoices that he is our Savior. Thus there is a joyful relationship between us and the Trinity and between us and the incarnate Lord and the risen Christ, five great joys.

During the span of our earthly life, we experience an extraordinary mixture of happiness and sorrow. The risen Lord Jesus abides in us. We also possess the fallen and wretched nature of the sinful Adam. By Adam's sin, we are broken in so many ways and are in so much pain that we can scarcely find any comfort. By Christ, we are touched and kept in grace and raised to a sure hope of salvation. We experience now the one, now the other.

Yet with all of this, God works in us by his mercy and grace, to have an abiding intention to remain in him. His love opens the eye of our understanding by which we see, sometimes more, sometimes less, according as God gives us the ability. Now we are raised into the one which gives us joy. Now we are suffered to fall into the other which is a vale of tears. This mixture is so extraordinary that we scarcely know where we or our fellow Christians stand. We do feel that God gives us a holy assent to himself with all our heart and soul and might. It is he who directs and sets our will to abide with him. Some Christians see this as a fundamental option for God which remains with us through thick and thin. By means of this option, inspired by faith, we remain united to God in love even in the face of most spiritual or moral failings. This is our comfort, that our assent is given to Christ by the power of his Holy Spirit, and even when we experience the pain of our fallings, we are preserved in his grace and mercy.

We do have reason to mourn as we see that our sins have been the cause of Christ's sufferings. Yet, we also have reason to rejoice as we see that his endless love caused him to embrace those sufferings. In this life, we will not be entirely free from sin. We can by grace be freed from mortal sins, and we can, reasonably and according to our ability, often avoid venial sins. If we fall through our weakness, we can readily arise, knowing the sweet touch of God's grace, and go forth to God in love without giving in to despair on the one side, or presumption on the other. We admit our feebleness and cling to God. God sees things in one way and man sees them in another. It is man's place to see his own truth and humbly accuse himself. It is God's place, out of his love and goodness, to excuse man. God thus brings us honor instead of blame, pity instead of guilt.

Our very weaknesses are gifts from God as are our strengths. Thus everything, everything, everything is a grave. As God is the ground of our being, he is behind all our wiles and woes, supporting us with his grace and mercy.

Jesus cried from the cross, "Why have you forsaken me?" The very fact that he could address such a cry to his Father meant that the Father had not forsaken him at all, but was, indeed, the very source of that cry. As a man, Jesus was led to acknowledge his feebleness and cry to the Father for grace and mercy. The ultimate response to Jesus' plea is found in his last words on the cross, "Father, into your hands, I commend my spirit."

It is all right for us, and sometimes even necessary, to cry out to the Lord, to voice our feelings of abandonment. The Lord will respond and we will be made strong in our weaknesses.

Chapter 25
God and Us

From Shewings- Chapter 54

We are so united to God that we can be said to become God. Is there any difference between us and God? Yes and no! God is God and we are creatures in God. He made us and not we ourselves. Yet, we exist only by reason of God's very being and we continue to exist only by reason of God's holding us in existence. So great and intimate is our oneness with God! The great truth of the Trinity is that God is our Father, for he made us and protects us in himself. The deep wisdom of the Trinity is that the second person is our Mother, in whom we are all enclosed. The high goodness of the Trinity is the Holy Spirit, our Lord, in whom we are enclosed and who is enclosed in us. We are enclosed in the Father, we are enclosed in the Son, and we are enclosed in the Holy Spirit. Yet the Father is enclosed in us and the Son is enclosed in us and the Holy Spirit is enclosed in us.

This is not a superficial or accidental oneness but a substantial union with the Trinity who shares with us something of his very being by way of creation and love. Our faith, which comes to us from the Holy Spirit, gives us a right understanding, true belief and a sure trust that we are in God and God is in us. Through this faith, God works in us great things. We respond to him by the working of the Holy Spirit who re-creates us in the image and likeness of our mothering Christ.

Prayer allows us to lift up our hearts to God with a gentle stirring of love, desiring him for his own sake and not for his gifts. This is the ultimate expression of union with God. At times, of course, we have an awareness of our personal needs, and the needs of others. We should express these needs to God in prayer. We need to ask God to give us our daily bread, to forgive us our trespasses and to lead us on the narrow pathway to his kingdom. At other times though, through God's grace and mercy, we will realize that the only thing that matters is God's will. May his will become the fullness of our prayer. This will be our expression and our experience of God as all in all. God will be more than mother, father, spouse and savior. He will be beyond what any words or any relationship can express. He will be our all!

Chapter 26

Dwelling in Heaven

From Shewings- Chapters 55 to 56

Christ is our way, leading us by his teachings. He is also our way by taking us into heaven with himself. When he ascended, Christ presented to his Father the human race he died to save. This was received with joy by the Father, with bliss by the Son and with pleasure by the Holy Spirit. In spite of our earthly feelings of alternate happiness and grief, God wants us to understand and believe that our dwelling is more truly in Heaven than on earth.

When we were created, God gave us the clear light of reason, the natural love of our heart and a steadfast mind. From all this comes our faith. When God breathed a soul into our bodies, we became sensual persons. (Our soul did not actually preexist our body but it did exist in the mind of God from all eternity -- as did all of his acts of creation.) It was at our creation that mercy and grace began to work, caring for us with pity and love bestowed by the Holy Spirit. Thus we are grounded, not only in nature, but also in mercy and grace, gifts which lead to endless life. We are in God and God is in us and always will be. We are in Christ who shares our humanity and Christ is in us who are given to share in his divinity.

St. Therese tells us that the way to heaven is heaven. We already have that for which we seek. This is because the Lord of bliss dwells within us. He is the ground of our being which makes celestial joy an intimate part of who we are. St. Augustine says that a Christian should be alleluia! from head to foot.

This joy consists in a deep abiding sense of our intimacy with God. It is always present even when we are undergoing the sufferings of our crosses and the mourning and weeping all too often present in this vale of tears.

We live in the era of the Holy Spirit whom Jesus has sent to us as a comforter. As the poet, Hopkins says, "the Holy Ghost broods over the bent world with warm breast and bright wings." This joy, this comfort is ours to have if we but freely choose it. If we do not freely choose God and the joy of his Holy Spirit then, by default we choose the frustration, pain and despair of the world, the flesh and the devil. What folly this would be. As Joshua told the ancient Jews, "I place before you this day good and evil, life and death, choose good that you and your children may live."

Chapter 27
Knowing God

From Shewings- Chapters 56 to 57

God is nearer to us than our own soul but we can never come to full knowing of God until we first clearly know our own soul. Humility, knowledge of self, is foundational to knowledge of God. God is nearer to us than we are to ourselves. In one way, because our soul is so deep grounded in God, we are more apt to come to the knowledge of God than to the knowledge of our own soul. To truly know our own soul, we must seek it where it is, and that is in God. But whether the Holy Spirit stirs us to know God or our own soul, we should know them both as united together.

God is the ground in whom our soul stands. He is the cause that keeps our body and soul together. Our soul rests in God, is strengthened in God and is rooted in his endless love. To come to the full knowledge of God, we must know our own soul. We must know it as touched by God, as grounded in God and as the recipient of his mercy and grace. To know this, is to know our soul and to know our soul in this way is to know God.

Our soul was created in the image and likeness of the Blessed Trinity. It has memory which is able to recall something of the Father who created it. It has understanding which resembles the wisdom of the Son. It has goodness which images the love of the Holy Spirit. The excellence and dignity of these three powers of the soul was lost by Adam, and by us, when he opted instead for love and delight in himself and other created things. Although we cannot, in this life, recover fully this threefold image of God, we are blessed with the desire to do so. We can do this by God's grace, but in an imperfect manner. Only in heaven will the image be perfectly restored.

We must seek then for that which is lost in Adam. We will be given a spiritual eye to see at least some small part of the dignity and beauty we were given at our creation and which we can have again by grace. This inward sight will prompt us to loathe in our heart our fallen self and see those created things we have chosen over God.

There is one name by which we may seek, desire and find that original dignity. In this name is everything that we have lost. The name is Jesus. It is not merely a word such as one writes on paper or sees in print, but is a desire for the reality behind that name. In our contemplative prayer, we grasp that reality, which is really God, by means of the Holy Spirit who gives us a spiritual power which turns that desire into a loving knowledge of Truth. To desire God is to love God. The power to do this comes only from God. Seek the Lord Jesus by this power and your desire will become love, affection, spiritual fervor, light and knowledge of truth. Set your desire on no other created thing. Let it be clothed, rested and anointed in Jesus. You will then be given to find something of Jesus, not him as he really is, but a shadow of him. The more you find Jesus in this way, the more you will desire him.

And then you must take note of what kind of prayer, or meditation, or exercise of devotion stirs up in you the greatest and surest desire and feeling for Jesus. Make a habit of this prayer so that you may find him. You had lost Jesus, but where? Like the woman who lost the coin, he is somewhere in your house, that is to say, in your soul. He has never been quite lost, though he seems lost to you. He is still within you, but you are not within him until you have found him again.

This is his graciousness that he suffers himself to be lost only where he may be found. There is no need to run to Rome or to Jerusalem to seek him there. Turn your attention into your own soul where the hidden God abides. The kingdom of heaven is within you. It is the treasure hidden in your field and you must give all that you have to possess it.

You must try to frame and shape yourself to be reformed in his likeness so that he may know you, come to you in an intimate way and reveal to you his secrets. The only way to reform yourself to his image and likeness is the way of humility and charity. This is how he will manifest himself to you. No virtue, no good work can make you like unto the Lord without humility and charity.

We can see clearly in the Gospels that these two virtues are the most acceptable to him. Our Lord speaks of humility in this way: Learn of me for I am meek and humble of heart. He does not say: Learn of me to go barefoot, or to go into the desert to fast, or to choose disciples, but rather: Learn of me for I am meek and humble of heart. Regarding charity, he says: This is my commandment that you love one another as I have loved you. It is by this that men shall know you are my disciples. Not that you work miracles, move mountains, cast out devils, or preach, but that you love one another. So if you will be reformed into Jesus, have humility and charity.

You know then what charity is: to love your neighbor as yourself. Now what is humility? How do we achieve it? You must enter into yourself, see the ground of sin within you and destroy as much of it as you can with God's help. Thus you will recover some part of your soul's lost dignity. Draw in your thoughts and make it your intention and purpose to seek within only the grace and spiritual presence of Jesus.

At times this will be painful because heavy and dark thoughts will press into your heart. A darkness will sometimes affect you and you will seem even to lose the possession of the name of Jesus. This darkness, coming from your subconscious, is the image of your own soul without the light or knowledge or feeling of the love of God. It is the beginning of humility. For this reason, the mystic, Walter Hilton, calls it a lightsome darkness. It will lead you back to Jesus. Knowledge of self is foundational to knowledge of God. St. Paul calls it a body of darkness and of sin. Through this darkness you will find a naked remembrance of the name of Jesus. Remember now that you call the Lord into your thoughts by your prayer word, against this darkness. Think then, on Jesus and his love because he is hidden in this darkness. You cannot find him with all your seeking until you pass through this darkness, through this cloud of unknowing. He will touch your soul and you will become a companion of St. Paul who cried out: Who shall deliver me from this body and this image of death? And he answered himself: The grace of God through Jesus Christ. In this way, by the finger of God, humility becomes charity and the image of sin becomes the likeness of God.

True humility almost forces us into charity. The truth about our self is that we were made for God and we cannot rest until we rest in God. Without God we are nothing. This nothingness, when realized and accepted, opens us up to our need for God and literally impels us to seek his mercy and grace. It is a painful movement from nothing to grace, but not without its joy and consolations. God does not abandon us, but rather is most with us in this suffering and this darkness. St. John of the Cross reminds us that the darkest part of the night is just before the dawn.

Chapter 28
The Maternal Jesus

From Shewings- Chapter 6

Sometimes even when we have advanced on our spiritual journey, God allows us to fall into sin in a way that seems worse than we have ever done before. And we, lacking wisdom, feel that all we have labored at spiritually up until now has been for nothing. But this is simply not true.

It was necessary for us to fall and to be keenly aware of it. It is the only way we can really know how feeble and wretched we are, left to ourselves. This, of course, is the virtue of humility and by this; we are given to know the marvelous love of God. Once we are in heaven, we will see clearly that we have sinned seriously during our earthly life, and yet, we will be given to see that this sin never lessened God's love for us nor did it diminish our value in God's eyes. By this recognition of our failures, we are given a truly marvelous understanding of God's love. Strong and wonderful, indeed, is that love which may not or will not be broken because of our offenses. This knowledge of the truth, this humility, also gives us to realize better our own feebleness and lowliness which, in turn, leads us to understand that we shall be more highly raised in heaven than we would be had we never sinned. This raising is caused not by our sin, but by our humility in recognizing our sinfulness through the mercy of God.

A mother may sometimes allow her child to be hurt in some way or other so that the child may learn. But her love would never allow the child's life to be in danger. So Jesus, who has for us a heavenly, maternal love, will never allow us, his children, born of his suffering and death on the cross, to perish. He has the power of the Father, the wisdom of the Son, and the love of the Holy Spirit. Blessed be his name.

Often it does happen that when we are made aware of our failures, we are greatly ashamed of ourselves and even very much afraid. At times, we are so much at a loss that we don't know where to turn, or what to do. Then Jesus, like a loving mother, wants us to become as little children. He wants us, when we are hurt and afraid, to run to him as fast as we can. He wants us to pray like this: "Jesus, in your maternal love, pity me. I have sinned against heaven and you. Only with your help and grace can I make amends."

If we do not feel his comfort at once, we can be sure that, like a wise mother, he realizes that it is better for us for a while, to mourn and weep. He allows this with compassion until the time comes for the comfort of his love to show itself. Then he wills us to act like the child who, both in pain and in joy, naturally trusts in the love of its mother.

It is at times like this that Jesus wants us also to see holy Church is our mother, one with him, and he wants us to turn to her with faith. Alone, we may experience ourselves as broken, but together with the whole body of his Church, we never are and never will be broken. It is a sure thing for us to desire humbly but firmly to be united to our mother, holy Church, that is, Christ Jesus. Here Jesus takes on the role of a kind nurse who has nothing else to do but be concerned about the well-being of her child.

At the Eucharist, before receiving Holy Communion, we pray that God will not look upon our sins, but on the faith of the church. This faith is ours because we are the church. We are the Body of Christ, the bride without stain or wrinkle even as we protest our unworthiness. Holy things (the Eucharist) are for the holy and in the acknowledgment of our sins, we are made holy.

Chapter 29
Restored

From Shewings- Chapter 62

God is our father and mother and we, like everything else he has made, flow out of him to do his will. We shall be restored and returned to him by his grace. This is the meaning of salvation. It is through our sins that God shows us our frailty, afflictions, sorrows and woes. In this way, he shows us his might (as the Father), his wisdom (as the Son), and his love (as the Holy Spirit), which protects us in our sins and sinfulness as lovingly and as tenderly, to his honor and our salvation, as he does when we are experiencing his grace and comfort. His love allows nothing to be wasted, neither our time of shame and sorrow, nor our time of joy and comfort.

Of one thing we can be sure. God's love is abiding and stable. In shame and in joy, in sorrow and in comfort, the loving God is present to us. He is with us in weil as in woe. What a consolation this is. It is also the cause for us to realize the unconditional nature of God's love. We do not earn it. We do not deserve it. It is also a lesson for us, that as he has loved us so also should we love one another.

Chapter 30
Hope

From Shewings- Chapter 65

Try to understand that when a man or woman chooses God in this life with a firm and loving will, they in turn are loved by God. Even while we are here on earth, God wants us to be as confident in the hope of the bliss of heaven as we shall be in certainty when we are actually there. By reason of the virtue of hope, we already possess that for which we are hoping, namely God. The more pleasure and joy we take in this certainty, reverently and humbly, the better is God pleased. In this way, we see the greatness of God and the littleness of ourselves. God wants us to know that everything he has done for his creation, he has done for me. This is what binds me to him in love and to everything else. The love of God gives all creation such a unity that, when he realizes it, no man can ever see himself as separate from any other.

God reveals this to us so that we will love him and be concerned with nothing but him. Neither the forces of evil, nor the passions, nor bodily sickness, nor any figment of our imagination should concern us overmuch. We can be so totally taken up with these things that we seem to be feeling nothing but pain, sorrow and distress. But the knowledge and love of God will suddenly bring us peace and rest and his will, expressed in all that he does, shall bring us great joy.

Chapter 31
God in Us

From Shewings- Chapter 67

Jesus sits in regal glory in our souls as in his holy city in peace and rest. Even though he is the mighty triune God who rules heaven and earth as the Father with his unique power, as the Son with His unique wisdom, and as the Holy Spirit with his unique love, he resides in the individual soul as his most familiar and pleasant home which he will never abandon.

The Blessed Trinity took endless joy in creating man's soul because he saw from all eternity that it would please him forever. He made man's soul for himself and it cannot rest until it rests in him. We are able to recognize the glory that God has given to all creation beneath us, but we can never find there a resting place. We are able to recognize the glory God has given to our own souls, but we can never find there a resting place. It is only when we behold the glory of God dwelling in our own soul that we will find rest and peace.

We should take great pleasure in knowing that

God enjoys our souls as the pinnacle of his creation. If it were possible for God to have made our souls any fairer, any nobler, any better than he did, he could not have taken such pleasure in it. He wills that our hearts be powerfully raised above all earthly things and even above themselves and find joy only in him.

Chapter 32
The Gift of Faith

From Shewings- Chapters 68 to 71

God wants us to be confident that we shall never be overcome by forces contrary to his love. He does not say that we will not be tried, that we will not be burdened, that we will not be afflicted. What he does say is that we shall not be overcome. God wants us to be aware of this so that we will be strong in trusting him in bad times as well as good. Just as he loves and enjoys us, so he wants us to love and enjoy and trust in him. And all shall be well.

All of this comes to us by way of the gift of faith. It is a gift of God and not the fruit of our own efforts. We believe these things and take comfort in them and trust in them on his word. We shall not be overcome.

Our faith is challenged in many ways. Our blindness in these matters is a great trial, but God's help is never lacking. He helps us within and without with the spiritual understanding and true teaching that our faith receives from holy

Church. There is no help for the soul outside of faith. Thus it is by faith that the Lord keeps us. By his goodness and his working in us, we are made strong. It is precisely because our faith is put to the test that it deserves the reward God promises it. The Lord gives great joy to our souls. He takes pleasure in this and considers it his reward. That true lasting joy which is Jesus unites us to him and to each other.

Chapter 33
God in Us

From Shewings- Chapter 72

Our Lord God dwells in us. He embraces us in a tender love that will never desert us. He is nearer to us than our hearts can feel or our tongue can say. At the same time, we will never be free from weeping and mourning, from pain and sorrow, yet ever desiring to feel his presence. It is only in heaven that we will see him clearly in an abiding well-being that knows no grief.

In this life, we find ourselves both in joy and in grief. We are in joy because our Lord, through his great goodness, is so near to us. He is actually in us and we in him. We grieve because our spiritual sight is so blind and we are so burdened with the weight of our mortal flesh and the darkness of sin, that we cannot see our Lord with any clarity. Because of this obscurity, we can hardly trust in his love and believe in his care and regard for us. So there is no lack of mourning or weeping in this valley of tears.

Weeping does not refer to the shedding of tears

by our physical eyes. There is a more spiritual understanding to it. Our desire to seek God is so great that we would not be comforted with all the noble things God has created if they were given to us in exchange for entering into his joy. We shall continue in spiritual weeping and painful longing until we see the face of God. Our hearts cannot be truly at rest until then. All the pain that tongue can tell or heart can feel would be as nothing if we could see the blissful face of our Lord. Thus that blissful sight of God, holds the goal of all our pain and the fulfilling of all our joy.

Chapter 34
Sin and Fear

From Shewings- Chapters 73 to 74

There are some sinful activities that the Lord would have us realize and work to amend. Many men and women, for love of God, hate sin and dispose of themselves to do his will. Yet they are still inclined to these things because of their spiritual blindness and the weakness of the flesh. God wants us to be aware of these sins especially because they may not be as obvious as some of our more blatant faults. To help us, the Lord gives us the example of the patience he had in his own sufferings, as well as the joy and satisfaction he received from those same loving sufferings. He shows us by his example that we should gladly and wisely bear our pains. This is greatly pleasing to him and endlessly profitable to us. Our sufferings are so burdensome because of our lack of understanding of his love.

It is true that the three persons of the Trinity possess, without limit, every good and blessed quality. But God wants that we especially understand, behold and enjoy his love! This is where our greatest failing lies. We believe that God is almighty and may do all things (the Father). We also believe that God is all wise and can do all things (the Son). But we stop short here and fail to understand that God is all love and will do all things (the Holy Spirit). This is the sin that hinders us most.

As we become more and more aware of our sins, we are often hindered by a fear that is so wearisome and shameful that we are totally devoid of comfort. Sometimes we take this fear for humility. Humility, however, is knowledge of the truth about ourselves and the truth is that we are not at all devoid of comfort. To think we are without comfort is a foul blindness and contrary to the truth. It is in itself a sin.

It is God's will that of all the gifts and comforts we receive, the one we should have the most confidence in is love. It is this love (from the Holy Spirit) that makes the power (from the Father) and the wisdom (from the Son) most perfect in us. God forgives our sin the moment we repent of it (even before that!). He wills that we too should forgive ourselves.

There is a kind of fear that is holy and does

come from God. We call this reverential fear. Of this the Scripture speaks by saying the fear of God is the foundation of wisdom. Reverential fear is pleasing to God. It is not painful to us because the stronger it is, the less we feel it, due to the comfort it brings us from love. Love and reverential fear are brothers and are rooted in us by the goodness of God. They shall never be taken from us. We are rooted in love by our very nature. We also are rooted in love by reason of God's grace. So it is by means of nature and grace that we are rooted in reverential fear, the brother of love. We should greatly desire that our Lord grace us with reverential fear, humble love and powerful trust. The more we trust him, the more we please and honor the Lord. If our fear and love is weak, so will be our trust. It is important then that we pray to our gracious Lord for reverential fear and humble love. Without these things no one can please him.

Chapter 35
Rise and Fall

From Shewings- Chapters 76 to 77

The soul that recognizes the loving kindness of our Lord Jesus is not concerned with hell but only with sin. Anyone who truly understands the teaching of the Holy Spirit hates sin for its vileness more than he despises all the pains of hell. So it is God's will that we be able to recognize sin and pray hard, work earnestly and seek humbly not to fall blindly into sin; and if we fall, that we rise readily. The most powerful reality that any soul may experience is to turn from God by sinning.

It is important to face our own sins and sinfulness, but when the sins of others come to mind, if we wish to remain in peace, we should flee those thoughts as we would the pains of hell. When we focus our attention on the sins of others, we create, as it were, a heavy mist before the eyes of our soul and are blinded to the gentleness of God. However, if we look on their sins with compassion and sorrow and a holy desire for their sakes, we do not obscure God's gentleness. Otherwise, the sins of others can do violence to our own souls.

The wisest thing anyone can do in this life is the will of the Lord. Do his will and follow his advice. His will and his advice is to unite ourselves to him firmly and comfortably in whatever moral shape we may be, whether it be holy or sinful. For good or for evil, it is his counsel that we never turn from him. Left to ourselves, we are fickle creatures and we often fall into sin. Then, due to our ignorance and blindness, we consider ourselves to be entirely wretched and unfaithful sinners. No matter how often we promise the Lord to do better, we fall again into the same errors. This makes us afraid to appear before our gentle Lord in prayer. This is a false fear, a fear of punishment and pain. It does not come from the Lord.

Our Lord wants us to know that anything in our life that is contrary to love and peace is from the world, the flesh, or the devil. Due to our weakness and folly, we will fail. But due to the mercy and grace of the Holy Spirit, we will rise again to an even greater joy. This is the remedy for all of our failures, that we be aware of our wretchedness and flee to the Lord. This is humility, to know the truth about ourselves and turn to the Lord for mercy and grace. The needier we are, the more deeply we have fallen and the quicker we should be to draw near to Jesus. We must also realize that God is almighty, all wise and all goodness and he loves us unconditionally. We must abide in this understanding for the mercy and grace of God works in us a lovely humility. Whatever chastening our Lord sends us will be light and easy if we only seek his will and follow his counsel.

Our sins may lead us to seek to do penance. A self-willed penance that we take upon ourselves is at best, questionable. A penance that is sent by the Lord should be humbly accepted and united to Christ's own sufferings and his blessed passion. Thus with pity and love, we can suffer with Christ like his friends did -- or should have. Our Lord wants us to beware of overdoing self-blame and thinking that all our tribulations are our own fault. He does not want us to be burdened with sorrow due to lack of judgment. We are going to have trials no matter what we do and it is the better part of wisdom to realize that our whole life is a salutary penance.

We must remember that the Lord is always with us in spite of our suffering, and indeed, because of our sufferings. He wants us to rejoice in the fact that this penitential life we must live is the prelude to the joys of heaven. Thus we are called to the practice of a joyful penance. Such a penance causes us to run to the Lord for comfort, to reach out and touch him to be made clean, and cling to him to be confident and safe from every spiritual danger.

Chapter 36
Four Things

From Shewings- Chapters 78 to 79

Our Lord is a merciful light by which we can see our feebleness. This feebleness is so pronounced that our Lord wants us to realize it only in the light of his mercy and grace. This is the virtue of humility. The Lord wants us to realize four things. First, he is the ground of our life and being. Second, by his power and mercy, he protects us while we are in sin and especially when we are in great spiritual danger because we do not realize our own desperate need. Third, he gently and respectfully watches over us and lets us realize that we are straying from the right path. Fourth, he faithfully abides with us even in our sin and wills that we turn to him again and be as one with him in love as he is with us. By this gracious knowledge, which is again the virtue of humility, we are able to see our sin profitably and yet without despair. It is necessary that we recognize our nothingness and feel a real shame for ourselves in order to escape our pride and presumption. Strangely enough, it is by showing us our littleness that the Lord reveals to us our greatness. He who humbles himself shall be exalted. Thus he leads us by grace to sorrow and contrition and breaks us away from all that is not himself. Our blessed Savior perfectly heals us and unites us to himself in love. The Lord puts before us, not punishment and hell, but love and forgiveness with the peace and joy that accompanies it.

All men and women are sinful and shall be so until the end of the world. God has enough comfort for us all. Each of us should be concerned for his own sin and not with the sins of others unless it be to comfort and help them.

We cannot trust in ourselves. We do not know how we shall sin nor how seriously. Our Lord wants us to know that his love for us is powerful, endless and will never change. Our souls can never be separated from his love. Our humility, our knowledge of the truth about our own feebleness, will save us from presumption. We will realize that God's steadfast love does not give us an excuse to be careless or even deliberate in committing sins. We need to be aware of the danger of reckless living or giving our hearts to anything less than God because of our assurance of God's love. Assurance of this kind is not from God.

When we fall, as we will, through ignorance or weakness, our gracious Lord touches and calls us so that we may be aware of our wretched condition. He does not want us to remain in that condition nor does he want us to overdo our guilt feelings, or our low self-esteem. He does want us to hasten to turn to him. He awaits us, for we are his joy and delight and he is our salvation.

Chapter 37
Three Ways

From Shewings- Chapters 80 to 81

We honor God in this life and hasten our journey towards the bliss of heaven in three ways. The first is by the use of natural means; the second is by the teachings of the Church; the third is by the inward workings of the Holy Spirit. To know these ways is a most valuable gift from God and is grounded in him. They continuously work together and provide us with great teachings which hasten our spiritual journey.

Our faith teaches us that God took upon himself our human nature and accomplished for us all that was needed for our salvation. He continues to dwell here with us and to govern and direct us in this life in order to bring us to eternal life with him in heaven. He will do this as long as it is necessary to save the very last soul of the human race. Love is never without pity. Whenever we forget Christ and fall into sin, the grief and woe that we are brought to feel is actually Christ in us. He is urging us to turn quickly to him as he awaits us. We are never alone no matter how often we fall from grace. He is always with us, always excusing us, and always shielding us from blame in his sight.

The Lord dwells in our soul. He wants us to rejoice more in this gracious presence than to mourn for our frequent fallings. The best kind of penance, the one that honors Christ the most, is that we live out our lives merrily and gladly because of his love. He gifts us with a natural attraction and longing for himself. This is our real penance: our striving for him. We will never be free from this penance until we finally have the Lord as our eternal reward. He desires that we now turn our hearts from the pain that we feel to the joy that we hoped for. St. Paul reminds us of this when he writes, "So we do not lose heart. Though our outer nature is wasting away, our inner nature is being renewed every day. For this slight momentary affliction is preparing for us an eternal weight of glory beyond all comparison."

Chapter 38
From Sin to Love

From Shewings- Chapter 82

Sin, of necessity, does bring about grief and pain. Even this comes from the Lord's love. The Lord looks on us, his servants, with pity and not with blame. We cannot live completely free from sin and blame in this passing life. God loves us endlessly and we sin almost routinely. He shows us this in his gentle fashion. As a result, we grieve and mourn, which makes us turn to him and cleave to him in his love and goodness. Through the humility, which comes from our awareness of our sinfulness, we get to know his eternal love. Then, we are led to thank and praise him, which pleases him greatly. So our sins with all their accompanying sorrow, pain and grief, lead us to a greater union with our Lord.

In our falling and rising we are continuously preserved in his love. When we see his love, we fall not and when we see our feebleness, we stand not. God wants to show us both our standing and our falling. He does want us, however, to be more aware of his grace and mercy than we are